STEM *trailblazer* BIOS

NASA
MATHEMATICIAN
KATHERINE JOHNSON

HEATHER E. SCHWARTZ

Lerner Publications ◆ Minneapolis

Lerner Publications Company
A division of Lerner Publishing Group, Inc.
241 First Avenue North
Minneapolis, MN 55401 USA

For reading levels and more information, look up this title at www.lernerbooks.com.

Content Consultant: James A. Flaten, Associate Director, NASA's Minnesota Space Grant Consortium

Library of Congress Cataloging-in-Publication Data

Names: Schwartz, Heather E.
Title: NASA mathematician Katherine Johnson / Heather E. Schwartz.
Description: Minneapolis : Lerner Publications, [2018] | Series: STEM trailblazer bios | Audience: Age 7–11. | Audience: Grade 4 to 6. | Includes bibliographical references and index.
Identifiers: LCCN 2016049263 (print) | LCCN 2016050364 (ebook) | ISBN 9781512457032 (lb : alk. paper) | ISBN 9781512457049 (pb : alk. paper) | ISBN 9781512457056 (eb pdf)
Subjects: LCSH: Johnson, Katherine G. | African American women mathematicians—Biography—Juvenile literature. | Mathematicians—United States—Biography—Juvenile literature. | African American teachers—Biography—Juvenile literature.
Classification: LCC QA29.J64 S39 2018 (print) | LCC QA29.J64 (ebook) | DDC 510.92 [B] —dc23

LC record available at https://lccn.loc.gov/2016049263

Manufactured in the United States of America
1-42953-26767-2/17/2017

The images in this book are used with the permission of: NASA, pp. 4, 12, 15, 16, 18, 21, 22, 23, 24, 25, 27; Courtesy of West Virginia State University, pp. 6, 8; The Dolph Briscoe Center for American History, University of Texas at Austin, p. 10; © Smith Collection/Gado/Archive Photos/Getty Images, p. 14; NASA/Bill Ingalls, p. 26.

Front cover: NASA

Main body text set in Adrianna Regular 13/22. Typeface provided by Chank.

CONTENTS

Chapter 1

Johnson at the NASA Langley Research Center in 1980

BRILLIANT BEGINNING

The world Katherine Johnson grew up in did not always honor women who excelled in math—especially African American women. When Katherine was young, women were expected to be homemakers, teachers, or nurses. African

Americans faced **discrimination** in all areas of life. But Katherine was born with a natural gift for numbers. Using her talent for math, she excelled in school. And she broke barriers in a career that put her to work as a brilliant mathematician, doing mathematical calculations that would later be done by computers.

GIRL WITH A GIFT

Katherine was born in White Sulphur Springs, West Virginia, in 1918. Her mother had been a teacher, and her father was a farmer and a custodian. He had not gone to school beyond the sixth grade. But he had a knack for working with numbers. When he cut lumber, he could calculate the number of boards he could get from a tree just by looking at it. He could also solve math problems that Katherine's teachers could not figure out.

Katherine seemed to have inherited that natural ability. As a child, she was always counting. She counted her steps when she walked to church. She counted plates and silverware when she washed dishes after meals.

When her older siblings Horace, Margaret, and Charles started school, Katherine was left behind—but not for long. She was allowed into summer school early because she could already read at a young age. At the age of five, she was put in second grade. This put her ahead of one older brother in school, and she breezed through the next few years of elementary school.

CIRCLE OF SUPPORT

By the age of ten, Katherine was ready for high school. Her town did not have a high school she could attend. But her father believed all of his kids should have an education. He made sure Katherine and her siblings went to high school in another town. The school was on the campus of West Virginia

Students pose on the campus of West Virginia State College, where Katherine attended high school in the 1930s.

State College in Institute, West Virginia. So Katherine and her siblings lived in Institute with their mother during the school year while their father stayed home and worked.

In high school, Katherine began getting even more attention for being an outstanding student. One of her favorite classes was geometry. Her teacher, Angie Turner King, acted as a **mentor** to Katherine and encouraged her to succeed. Katherine's school principal, Sherman H. Gus, was another mentor. He took the time to teach Katherine about the constellations. She began to develop an interest in **astronomy**. Still, Katherine did not imagine she would grow up to become an astronomer or a mathematician. She thought she would probably become a math teacher.

TECH TALK

"Math. It's just there. It has always been a part of whatever I was doing. You're either right or you're wrong. That I like about it."

—*Katherine Johnson*

Chapter 2

Katherine Johnson attended West Virginia State College (*above*), which later changed its name to West Virginia State University.

STAR
STUDENT

At only fourteen, Katherine graduated from high school. Then she attended West Virginia State College. In college, Katherine struggled to choose a major, or a main area of study. She loved math. But she loved French too. Her

mentors continued encouraging her to focus on math. One tough female math professor practically ordered Katherine to take her class. Another math professor, James Carmichael Evans, told her he respected her interest in French. But he too insisted that she stick with her math studies. Katherine knew he was right. But she figured out a way to keep up with French as well—she decided to major in both math and French!

Katherine also impressed a somewhat famous math professor at her college. W. W. Schieffelin Claytor was the third African American in the United States to earn a PhD in math. He encouraged Katherine to work toward becoming a research mathematician after graduation. In that career, she would use math to solve real-world problems.

INQUISITIVE MIND

Katherine was thrilled by the idea. Claytor made sure she studied the coursework that would prepare her to meet her new goal. He even created college courses with her in mind. In his course about the geometry of space, she was his only student.

In other classes, Katherine tried to help her fellow students. She could tell when her classmates did not understand the lesson. She would ask Claytor questions until he wondered

Claytor faced a lot of racism throughout his career. But he encouraged Katherine to pursue a career in mathematics.

why his star student didn't understand. She finally had to explain the purpose of her questions to him. Asking questions was a learning strategy Katherine would continue to use throughout her career.

In 1937, at the age of eighteen, Katherine graduated **summa cum laude**. She had two bachelor of science degrees: one in French and the other in math. But she did not become a research mathematician immediately. Instead, she followed a more traditional path for a woman of her time. She took teaching jobs and got married. She and her husband, James Goble, had three children together. Johnson also began graduate studies in math and physics at West Virginia University.

Chapter 3

Many women worked as mathematicians at NACA's Langley Research Center in Virginia.

LIFE-CHANGING CHANCE

Johnson was still working as a teacher when she went to a family party in the early 1950s. A relative there told her the National Advisory Committee for Aeronautics (NACA) was hiring mathematicians. The agency began hiring more women in 1941, when it lost many male workers to World War II (1939–1945). And in 1941, President Franklin Delano Roosevelt signed an order to prevent discrimination in the workplace, and NACA began hiring more African American women. NACA was working on research and creating new technology for flight, and they needed African American women to work as human computers—or people who completed calculations that would later be done by computers—for its male engineers. Johnson thought this seemed like an amazing opportunity. She applied immediately. But she was too late. The agency had already filled the positions. She had to wait another year to apply again. This time, she was successful. She gave up teaching to join NACA in 1953.

HUMAN COMPUTERS

At NACA, Johnson used a mechanical calculator and a slide rule to solve problems and check calculations for the engineers. A mechanical calculator was a large machine used for adding, subtracting, multiplying, and dividing. A slide rule was marked with numbers. A center strip slid to show answers to math problems.

Johnson was not always treated fairly in her new position. Women doing her job were not considered **professionals**.

Instead, their position was called subprofessional. As an African American, she also had to work in a **segregated** environment. White women and African American women did the same job, but the African American workers were in a separate building. They had their own bathroom and ate lunch at a table set aside for them. A cardboard sign declared the table was for "colored computers."

A group of human computers eats lunch together in 1950.

A woman works at NACA as a human computer. She has a large calculating machine on her desk.

Still, Johnson had a chance to use her math skills at NACA. Her husband died in 1956, and with a family to support, it helped that she was earning more money than she had as a teacher. Best of all, she was on a path toward even more opportunity.

NACA technicians prepare equipment in a wind tunnel, used to test aircraft on the ground.

CONTINUING TO QUESTION

Johnson was not a show-off. But since numbers came naturally to her, she did her job extremely well. And she didn't hide her intelligence. For her, that meant asking questions of the engineers who needed her calculations. She asked them about the problems she was working on. She didn't just want to calculate. She wanted to know more about what the engineers were trying to do. She also asked them why women never attended the engineers' meetings. She asked them if there was a law against it. As it turned out, there wasn't.

TECH TALK

"The women did what they were told to do. They didn't ask questions or take the task any further. I asked questions; I wanted to know why. They got used to me asking questions and being the only woman there."

—*Katherine Johnson*

Chapter 4

The first seven NASA astronauts pose for a photo in 1959. Johnson worked to send the first American astronauts into space.

LEADER
AMONG MEN

NACA's engineers recognized Johnson's intelligence. Because she asked questions, she earned their respect. She also earned the opportunity to attend the engineers' meetings. None of the other women she worked with joined the meetings.

Five years after she started at the agency, NACA became the National Aeronautics and Space Administration (NASA). Johnson was promoted to the Space Task Force. The task force had to figure out how to send American astronauts to outer space. In her new job, Johnson used geometry to plan how spacecraft should travel. She was the only female and the only African American member of the task force, and she continued asking questions and speaking up. She emerged as a leader of the group. The other members knew they needed her.

One time, a report needed to be finished, but the men working on it ran out of time. Johnson completed the report and included her own research about launching, tracking, and

READY, SET, SPACE RACE

The United States became more interested in space travel after the Soviet Union (a nation that existed from 1922–1991, based in modern-day Russia) launched the first spacecraft into orbit in 1957. That event started a space race between the two countries as each country competed to improve space exploration technology and put a man on the moon.

returning spacecraft to Earth. It was the first time a woman's name appeared on a report from the Flight Research Division of NASA.

ACE IN SPACE

Katherine Johnson married James A. Johnson, a US military officer, in 1959. She continued her career with NASA, and in May 1961, the United States sent its first astronaut, Alan Shepard, into outer space. He made history, and Johnson was part of it. Behind the scenes, she was responsible for calculating the path of his flight. She used geometry to determine the spacecraft's height, speed, and landing location.

By 1962, NASA was using machines to perform calculations. But when American astronaut John Glenn was set to go on his

TECH TALK

"Everything was so new—the whole idea of going into space was new and daring. There were no textbooks, so we had to write them. . . . We created the equations needed to track a vehicle in space."

—Katherine Johnson

space mission, he was skeptical. He trusted Johnson more than he trusted the machines. He asked her to check the numbers. She found that they were correct, and Glenn became the first American to orbit Earth.

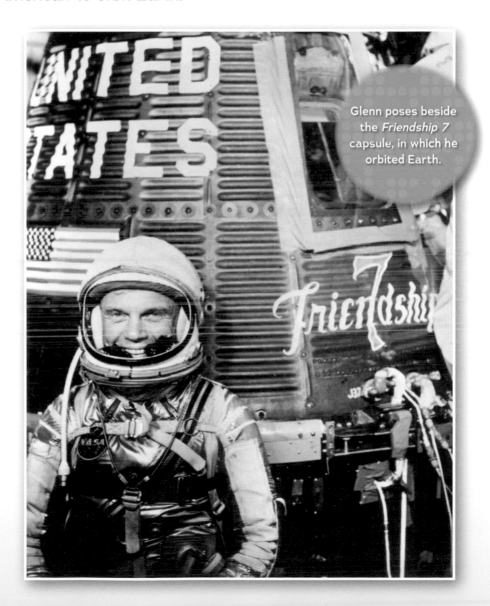

Glenn poses beside the *Friendship 7* capsule, in which he orbited Earth.

Chapter 5

Johnson performing calculations

WOMAN ON A MISSION

In 1969, Johnson was part of the mission she was most proud of throughout her career. The Apollo 11 mission was America's first manned mission to land astronauts on the surface of the moon. Johnson calculated the path that would

take astronauts Neil Armstrong, Edwin E. "Buzz" Aldrin Jr., and Michael Collins to the moon.

Johnson had to be sure to properly calculate the position of Earth in relation to the moon. She had to figure in how these positions would change due to Earth's motion in orbit around the sun and the moon's motion in orbit around Earth while the spacecraft was in flight. She also had to figure in the speed of the spacecraft on its way to the moon. But she was more concerned about the trip back to Earth. The calculations were

Left to right: Armstrong, Collins, and Aldrin were all experienced astronauts before completing the Apollo 11 mission.

very precise. She knew she had to depend on the astronauts to use their instruments properly to get into orbit. If they were just one degree off, there would be major problems. Throughout the mission, she hoped everything would go right, including her calculations.

On July 20, Armstrong and Aldrin landed on the surface of the moon. Collins stayed in orbit around the moon. The three astronauts returned safely to Earth four days later. They brought back special keepsakes for Johnson and the members of her team: American flags that had been to the moon.

Aldrin walks on the surface of the moon.

HONORED FOR HER WORK

Throughout the 1960s, Johnson worked to create backup solutions in case of problems such as a computer failure or a loss of contact between a spacecraft and ground control. Her dedication motivated her to work sixteen hours a day—until she fell asleep while driving and decided she needed to make a change.

Johnson at the NASA Langley Research Center in 1971

Johnson wears her **Presidential Medal of Freedom.**

Johnson retired from NASA in 1986. For many years, her contributions to the US space program were not widely known. But in 2015, at the age of ninety-seven, she was awarded the Presidential Medal of Freedom, an honor given each year to inspiring people who have contributed to America's progress through cultural or national endeavors. In 2016, NASA opened the Katherine G. Johnson Computational Research Facility in her honor. That same year, author Margot Lee Shetterly told the story of Johnson and other women human computers in her book *Hidden Figures*. A movie based on the book was released in 2016.

Johnson poses for a photo with astronaut Leland Melvin at the naming event for the Katherine G. Johnson Computational Research Facility.

Johnson broke barriers as a female and African American mathematician. Her work contributed to the space age and helped the United States win the space race. But for her, the job was all about teamwork rather than winning credit. Using her natural talents led naturally to her success.

TECH TALK

"I never took any credit because we always worked as a team; it was never just one person."

—*Katherine Johnson*

TIMELINE

1918

Katherine is born.

1937

She graduates from West Virginia State College.

1953

She joins NACA.

1957

The Soviet Union sends an unmanned satellite into orbit around Earth.

1958

Johnson is promoted to the Space Task Force.

1969

American astronauts use Johnson's calculations on a mission to the moon and back.

2015

Johnson is awarded the Presidential Medal of Freedom.

2016

NASA names a new research facility in her honor.

SOURCE NOTES

7 "Here's What You Need to Know about the Real Women behind the 'Hidden Figures' Movie," *Makers*, August 16, 2016, http://www.makers.com/katherine-g-johnson.

17 Heather S. Deiss, "Katherine Johnson: A Lifetime of STEM," NASA, November 6, 2013, https://www.nasa.gov/audience/foreducators/a-lifetime-of-stem.html.

20 "Johnson, Katherine Coleman Goble," *Encyclopedia.com*, accessed December 5, 2016, http://www.encyclopedia.com/education/news-wires-white-papers-and-books/johnson-katherine-coleman-goble.

28 Meghan Bartels, "The Unbelievable Life of the Forgotten Genius Who Turned Americans' Space Dreams into Reality," *Business Insider*, August 22, 2016, http://www.businessinsider.com/katherine-johnson-hidden-figures-nasa-human-computers-2016-8.

GLOSSARY

astronomy
the scientific study of stars, planets, and other objects in outer space

discrimination
the practice of unfairly treating one group of people differently from other people

mentor
someone who teaches and gives advice to a younger, less experienced person

orbit
the curved path of an object such as a spacecraft, around something such as a planet or a moon

professionals
people who hold jobs that require education, training, and skill

segregated
separated by race

summa cum laude
an honor given to students who have graduated at the highest level of achievement in college

FURTHER INFORMATION

BOOKS

Calkhoven, Laurie. *Women Who Changed the World: 50 Amazing Americans*. New York: Scholastic, 2016. Find out about more women who used their skills to change the world.

Di Piazza, Domenica. *Space Engineer and Scientist Margaret Hamilton*. Minneapolis: Lerner Publications, 2018. Read all about another woman who worked behind the scenes to put humans on the moon.

Shetterly, Margot Lee. *Hidden Figures: Young Readers' Edition*. New York: HarperCollins, 2016. Learn more about the African American human computers hired to help win the space race.

WEBSITES

National Geographic Kids: "Black Inventors and Pioneers of Science"
http://kids.nationalgeographic.com/explore/science/black
-inventors-and-pioneers-of-science/#black-scientist-jemison.jpg
Meet more inspiring African American scientists and inventors.

Women at JPL
http://www.jpl.nasa.gov/women/grid.html
Read about some women who currently work for NASA, including one who started as a human computer in 1958.

LERNER
SOURCE

Expand learning beyond the printed book. Download free, complementary educational resources for this book from our website, www.lernerresource.com.

INDEX

ABOUT THE AUTHOR

Heather E. Schwartz has written more than sixty nonfiction books for kids. She always enjoys researching and learning about people who have a passion for what they do, such as Katherine Johnson.